The SUPERNATURAL WAYS of ROYALTY

LEADER'S GUIDE

DESTINY IMAGE BOOKS BY KRIS VALLOTTON

Supernatural Ways of Royalty

Developing a Supernatural Lifestyle

Basic Training for the Prophetic Ministry

The *The* SUPERNATURAL
WAYS *of*
ROYALTY

LEADER'S GUIDE

*Discovering your rights and privileges
of being a son or daughter of God*

KRIS VALLOTTON

Leader's Guide prepared by Enliven Media

DESTINY IMAGE® PUBLISHERS, INC.
P.O. Box 310, Shippensburg, PA 17257-0310
"Promoting Inspired Lives."

This book and all other Destiny Image and Destiny Image Fiction books are available at Christian bookstores and distributors worldwide.

Interior design by Terry Clifton

For more information on foreign distributors, call 717-532-3040.
Reach us on the Internet: www.destinyimage.com.

ISBN 13 TP: 978-0-7684-1581-0

For Worldwide Distribution, Printed in the U.S.A.
1 2 3 4 5 6 7 8 / 21 20 19 18 17

CONTENTS

Basic Leader Guidelines

This study is designed to help you develop into a believer who can go through any difficult situation and maintain a heavenly attitude and perspective. From this perspective, you will partner with God to see impossibilities bow at Jesus' name and step into the destiny God has for you!

There are several different ways that you can engage this study. By no means is this forthcoming list comprehensive. Rather, these are the standard outlets recommended to facilitate this curriculum. We encourage you to seek the Lord's direction, be creative, and prepare for supernatural transformation in your Christian life.

When all is said and done, this curriculum is unique in that the end goal is *not* information—it is transformation. The sessions are intentionally sequenced to take every believer on a journey from information, to revelation, to transformation. Participants will receive a greater understanding of what partnership with Heaven looks like and learn how to practically live this supernatural lifestyle on a daily basis.

Here are some of the ways you can use the curriculum:

1. Church Small Group

Often, churches feature a variety of different small group opportunities per season in terms of books, curriculum resources, and Bible studies. *Supernatural Ways of Royalty* would be included among the offering of titles for whatever season you are launching for the small group program.

It is recommended that you have at least four to five people to make up a small group and a maximum of twelve. If you end up with more than 12 members, either the group needs to multiply and break into two different groups or you should consider moving toward a church class model (which will be outlined below).

For a small group setting, here are the essentials:

* *Meeting place*: Either the leader's home or a space provided by the church.
* *Appropriate technology*: A DVD player attached to a TV that is large enough for all of the group members to see (and loud enough for everyone to hear).

- *Leader/Facilitator*: This person will often be the host, if the small group is being conducted at someone's home; but it can also be a team (husband/wife, two church leaders, etc.). The leader(s) will direct the session from beginning to end, from sending reminder e-mails to participating group members about the meetings, to closing out the sessions in prayer and dismissing everyone. That said, leaders might select certain people in the group to assist with various elements of the meeting—worship, prayer, ministry time, etc. A detailed description of what the group meetings should look like will follow in the pages to come.

Sample Schedule for Home Group Meeting (for a 7:00 P.M. Meeting)

- Before arrival: Ensure that refreshments are ready by 6:15 P.M. If they need to be refrigerated, ensure they are preserved appropriately until 15 minutes prior to the official meeting time.

- 6:15 P.M.: Leaders arrive at meeting home or facility.

- 6:15–6:25 P.M.: Connect with hosts, co-hosts, and/or co-leaders to review the evening's program.

- 6:25–6:35 P.M.: Pray with hosts, co-hosts, and/or co-leaders for the evening's events. Here are some sample prayer directives:

  - For the Holy Spirit to move and minister freely.

  - For the teaching to connect with and transform all who hear it.

  - For dialogue and conversation that edifies.

  - For comfort and transparency among group members.

  - For the Presence of God to manifest during worship.

  - For testimonies of answered prayers.

  - For increased hunger for God's Presence and power.

- 6:35–6:45 P.M.: Ensure technology is functioning properly!

  - Test the DVDs featuring the teaching sessions, making sure they are set up to the appropriate session.

  - If you are doing praise and worship, ensure that either the MP3 player or CD player is functional, set at an appropriate volume (not soft, but not incredibly loud), and that song sheets are available for everyone so they can sing along with the lyrics. (If you are tech savvy, you could do a PowerPoint or Keynote presentation featuring the lyrics.)

- 6:45–7:00 P.M.: Welcome and greeting for guests.

- 7:00–7:10 P.M.: Fellowship, community, and refreshments.

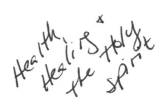

- 7:10–7:12 P.M.: Gather everyone together in the meeting place.

- 7:12–7:30 P.M.: Introductory prayer and worship.

- 7:30–7:40 P.M.: Ministry and prayer time.

- 7:40–8:00 P.M.: Watch DVD session.

- 8:00–8:20 P.M.: Discuss DVD session.

- 8:20–8:35 P.M.: Activation time.

- 8:35–8:40 P.M.: Closing prayer and dismiss.

This sample scheduled is *not* intended to lock you into a formula. It is simply provided as a template to help you get started. Our hope is that you customize it according to the unique needs of your group and sensitively navigate the activity of the Holy Spirit as He uses these sessions to supernaturally transform the lives of every person participating in the study.

2. SMALL GROUP CHURCH-WIDE CAMPAIGN

This would be the decision of the pastor or senior leadership of the church. In this model, the entire church would go through *Supernatural Ways of Royalty* in both the main services and ancillary small groups/life classes.

This campaign could be marketed as *50 Days to Identity.* The pastor's weekend sermon would be based on the principles in *Supernatural Ways of Royalty,* and the Sunday school classes/life classes and/or small groups would also follow the *Supernatural Ways of Royalty* curriculum format.

3. CHURCH CLASS | MID-WEEK CLASS | SUNDAY SCHOOL CURRICULUM

Churches of all sizes offer a variety of classes purposed to develop members into more effective disciples of Jesus and agents of transformation in their spheres of influence.

Supernatural Ways of Royalty would be an invaluable addition to a church's class offering. Typically, churches offer a variety of topical classes targeted at men's needs, women's needs, marriage, family, finances, and various areas of Bible study.

Supernatural Ways of Royalty is a unique resource, as it does not fit in with the aforementioned traditional topics usually offered to the church body. On the contrary, this study breaks down what it means to discover your rights and privileges as a child and shows believers how to live from a royal identity as a joint heir with Christ.

While it may be difficult to facilitate dialogue in a class setting, it is certainly optional and recommended. The other way to successfully engage *Supernatural Ways of Royalty* in a class setting is to have a teacher/leader go through the questions/answers presented in the upcoming pages and use these as his or her teaching notes.

4. Individual Study

While the curriculum is designed for use in a group setting, it also works as a tool that can equip anyone who is looking to strengthen his or her spirit and soul.

NOTES

NOTES

Steps to Launching a *Supernatural Ways of Royalty* Group or Class

Prepare with Prayer!

Pray! If you are a **church leader**, prayerfully consider how *Supernatural Ways of Royalty* could transform the culture and climate of your church community! The Lord is raising up bodies of believers who bring transformation in their wake because of the overflow of a mind that's been reoriented to Heaven's perspective. Spend some time with the Holy Spirit, asking Him to give you vision for what this unique study will do for your church, and, ultimately, how a Kingdom-minded people will transform your city and region.

If you are a **group leader** or **class facilitator**, pray for those who will be attending your group, signing up for your class, and positioning their lives to be transformed by the power and Presence of God in this study.

Prepare Practically!

Determine how you will be using the Supernatural Ways of Royalty curriculum.

Identify which of the following formats you will be using the curriculum in:

* Church-sponsored small group study
* Church-wide campaign
* Church class (Wednesday night, Sunday morning, etc.)
* Individual study

Determine a meeting location and ensure availability of appropriate equipment.

Keep in mind the number of people who may attend. You will also need AV (audio-visual) equipment. The more comfortable the setting, the more people will enjoy being there, and will spend more time ministering to each other!

A word of caution here: the larger the group, the greater the need for co-leaders or assistants. The ideal small group size is difficult to judge; however, once you get more than 10 to 12 people, it becomes difficult for each member to feel "heard." If your group is larger than 12 people, consider either having two or more small group discussion leaders or "multiplying" the larger group into two smaller ones.

Determine the format for your meetings.

The Presence of the Lord, which brings transformation, is cradled and stewarded well in the midst of organization. Structure should never replace spontaneity; on the contrary, having a plan and determining what type of format your meetings will take enables you to flow with the Holy Spirit and minister more effectively.

Also, by determining what kind of meeting you will be hosting, you become well equipped to develop a schedule for the meeting, identify potential co-leaders, and order the appropriate number of resources.

Set a schedule for your meetings.

Once you have established the format for your meetings, set a schedule for your meetings. Some groups like to have a time of fellowship or socializing (either before or after the meeting begins) where light refreshments are offered. Some groups will want to incorporate times of worship and personal ministry into the small group or class. This is highly recommended for *Supernatural Ways of Royalty*, as the study is designed to be founded upon equipping and activating believers through encountering God's Presence. The video portion and discussion questions are intended to instruct believers, while the worship, times of ministry, group interaction, prayer time, and activation elements are purposed to engage them to live out what they just learned. *Supernatural Ways of Royalty* is not a lofty theological concept; it is a practical reality to create a royal identity for every born-again believer. This study is intended to educate; but even more so, it is designed to activate believers and position them to steward their private, interior lives.

Establish a start date along with a weekly meeting day and time.

This eight-week curriculum should be followed consistently and consecutively. Be mindful of the fact that while there are eight weeks of material, most groups will want to meet one last time after completing the last week to celebrate, or designate their first meeting as a time to get to know each other and "break the ice." This is very normal and should be encouraged to continue the community momentum that the small group experience initiates. Typically, after the final session is completed, groups will often engage in a social activity—either going out to dinner together, seeing a movie, or something of the like.

Look far enough ahead on the calendar to account for anything that might interfere. Choose a day that works well for the members of your group. For a church class, be sure to coordinate the time with the appropriate ministry leader.

Advertise!

Getting the word out in multiple ways is most effective. Print out flyers, post a sign-up sheet, make an announcement in church services or group meetings, send out weekly e-mails and text messages, set up your own blog or website, or post the event on the social media avenue you and your group utilize most (Facebook, Twitter, etc.). A personal invitation or phone call is a great way to reach those who might need that little bit of extra encouragement to get involved.

For any type of small group or class to succeed, it must be endorsed by and encouraged from the leadership. For larger churches with multiple group/class offerings, it is wise to provide church members literature featuring all of the different small group/class options. This information should also be displayed online in an easily accessible page on your church website.

For smaller churches, it is a good idea for the pastor or a key leader to announce the launch of a small group course or class from the pulpit during an announcement time.

Gather your materials.

Each leader will need the *Supernatural Ways of Royalty's* Kit, as well as the *Supernatural Ways of Royalty* book.

Additionally, each participant will need a personal copy of the *Supernatural Ways of Royalty* workbook. It is recommended they also purchase the *Supernatural Ways of Royalty* book for further enrichment and as a resource to complement their daily readings. However, they are able to engage in the exercises and participate in the group discussion apart from reading the book.

We have found it best for the materials to all be purchased at one time—many booksellers and distributors offer discounts on multiple orders, and you are assured that each member will have their materials from the beginning of the course.

STEP FORWARD!

Arrive at your meeting in *plenty* of time to prepare; frazzled last-minute preparations do not put you in a place of "rest," and your group members will sense your stress! Ensure that all AV equipment is working properly and that you have ample supplies for each member. Nametags are a great idea, at least for the first couple of meetings. Icebreaker and introduction activities are also a good idea for the first meeting.

Pray for your members. As much as possible, make yourself available to them. As members increase in insight on strengthening themselves in the Lord, they will want to share that discovery! You will also need to encourage those who struggle, grow weary, or lose heart along the journey and through the process. Make sure your members stay committed so they experience the full benefits of this teaching.

Embrace the journey that you and your fellow members are embarking on to discover your rights and privileges as a child of God. Transformation begins within *you*!

Multiply yourself. Is there someone you know who was not able to attend your group? Help them to initiate their own small group now that you know how effective hosting *Supernatural Ways of Royalty* can be in a group setting!

Thank You

Thank you for embarking on a journey to equip the bride of Christ to be strong, peaceful, joyful, and who she is destined to be in this world.

Leader Checklist

One to Two Months Prior

_____ Have you determined a start date for your class or small group?

_____ Have you determined the format, meeting day and time, and weekly meeting schedule?

_____ Have you selected a meeting location (making sure you have adequate space and AV equipment available)?

_____ Have you advertised? Do you have a sign-up sheet to ensure you order enough materials?

Three Weeks to One Month Prior

_____ Have you ordered materials? You will need a copy of *Supernatural Ways of Royalty* Leader's Kit, along with copies of the workbook and book for each participant.

_____ Have you organized your meeting schedule/format?

One to Two Weeks Prior

_____ Have you received all your materials?

_____ Have you reviewed the DVDs and your Leader's Kit to familiarize yourself with the material and to ensure everything is in order?

_____ Have you planned and organized the refreshments, if you are planning to provide them? Some leaders will handle this themselves, and some find it easier to allow participants to sign up to provide refreshments if they would like to do so.

_____ Have you advertised and promoted? This includes sending out e-mails to all participants, setting up a Facebook group, setting up a group through your church's database system (if available), promotion in the church bulletin, etc.

_____ Have you appointed co-leaders to assist you with the various portions of the group/class? While it is not necessary, it is helpful to have someone who is in charge of either leading (on guitar, keyboard, etc.) or arranging the worship music (putting songs on a CD, creating song lyric sheets, etc.). It is also helpful to have a prayer coordinator as well—someone who helps facilitate the prayer time, ensuring that all of the prayer needs are acknowledged and remembered, and assigning the various requests to group members who are willing to lift up those needs in prayer.

First Meeting Day

_____ Plan to arrive *early!* Give yourself extra time to set up the meeting space, double check all AV equipment, and organize your materials. It might be helpful to ask participants to arrive 15 minutes early for the first meeting to allow for distribution of materials and any ice-breaker activity you might have planned.

NOTES

NOTES

Session Discussion Questions

Weekly Overview of Meetings/Group Sessions

Here are some instructions on how to use each of the weekly Discussion Question guides.

Welcome and Fellowship Time
(10–15 Minutes)

This usually begins five to ten minutes prior to the designated meeting time and typically continues up until ten minutes after the official starting time. Community is important. One of the issues in many small group/class environments is the lack of connectivity among the people. People walk around inspired and resourced, but they remain disconnected from other believers. Foster an environment where community is developed but, at the same time, not distracting. Distraction tends to be a problem that plagues small group settings more than classes.

Welcome: Greet everyone as they walk in. If it is a small group environment, as the host or leader, be intentional about connecting with each person as they enter the meeting space. If it is a church class environment, it is still recommended that the leader connect with each participant. However, there will be less pressure for the participants to feel connected immediately in a traditional class setting versus a more intimate small group environment.

Refreshments and materials: In the small group, you can serve refreshments and facilitate fellowship between group members. In a class setting, talk with the attendees and ensure that they purchase all of their necessary materials (workbook and optional copy of *Supernatural Ways of Royalty*). Ideally, the small group members will have received all of their resources prior to Week 1, but if not, ensure that the materials are present at the meeting and available for group members to pick up or purchase. It is advisable that you have several copies of the workbook and book available at the small group meeting, just in case people did not receive their copies at the designated time.

Call the meeting to order: This involves gathering everyone together in the appropriate place and clearly announcing that the meeting is getting ready to start.

Pray! Open every session in prayer, specifically addressing the topic that you will be covering in the upcoming meeting time. Invite the Presence of the Holy Spirit to come, move among the group members, minister to them individually, reveal Jesus, and stir greater hunger in each participant to experience *more* of God's power in their lives.

INTRODUCTIONS
(10 MINUTES—FIRST CLASS ONLY)

While a time of formal introduction should only be done on the first week of the class/session, it is recommended that in subsequent meetings group members state their names when addressing a question, making a prayer request, giving a comment, etc., just to ensure everyone is familiar with names. You are also welcome to do a short icebreaker activity at this time.

Introduce yourself and allow each participant to briefly introduce him/herself. This should work fine for both small group and class environments. In a small group, you can go around the room and have each person introduce himself/herself one at a time. In a classroom setting, establish some type of flow and then have each person give a quick introduction (name, interesting factoid, etc.).

Discuss the schedule for the meetings. Provide participants an overview of what the next eight weeks will look like. If you plan to do any type of social activity, you might want to advertise this right up front, noting that while the curriculum runs for eight weeks, there will be a ninth session dedicated to fellowship and some type of fun activity.

Distribute materials to each participant. Briefly orient the participants to the book and workbook, explaining the 10–15 minute time commitment for every day (Monday through Friday). Encourage each person to engage fully in this journey—they will get out of it only as much as they invest. The purpose for the daily reinforcement activities is *not* to add busywork to their lives. This is actually a way to cultivate a habit of Bible study and daily time renewing their minds, starting with just 10–15 minutes a day. Morning, evening, afternoon—*when* does not matter. The key is making the decision to engage.

WORSHIP

(15 MINUTES—OPTIONAL FOR THE FIRST MEETING)

Fifteen minutes is a solid time for a worship segment. That said, it all depends upon the culture of your group. If everyone is okay with doing 30 minutes of praise and worship, by all means, go for it!

For this particular curriculum, a worship segment is highly recommended, as true and lasting transformation happens as we continually encounter God's Presence.

If a group chooses to do a worship segment, usually they decide to begin on the second week. It often takes an introductory meeting for everyone to become acquainted with one another, and comfortable with their surroundings before they open up together in worship.

On the other hand, if the group members are already comfortable with one another and they are ready to launch immediately into a time of worship, they should definitely begin on the first meeting.

While it has been unusual for Sunday school/church classes to have a time of worship during their sessions, it is actually a powerful way to prepare participants to receive the truth being shared in the *Supernatural Ways of Royalty* sessions. In addition, pre-service worship (if the class is being held prior to a Sunday morning worship experience) actually stirs hunger in the participants for greater encounters with God's Presence, both corporately and congregationally.

If the class is held mid-week (or on a day where there is *no* church service going on), a praise and worship component is a wonderful way to refresh believers in God's Presence as they are given the privilege of coming together, mid-week, and corporately experiencing His Presence.

PRAYER/MINISTRY TIME

(5–15 MINUTES)

At this point, you will transition from either welcome or worship into a time of prayer.

Just like praise and worship, it is recommended that this initial time of prayer be five to ten minutes in length; but if the group is made up of people who do not mind praying longer, it should not be discouraged. The key is stewarding everyone's time well while maintaining focus on the most important things at hand.

Prayer should be navigated carefully, as there will always be people who use it as an opportunity to speak longer than necessary, vent about the circumstances in their lives, or potentially gossip about other people.

At the same time, there are real people carrying deep needs to the group and they need supernatural ministry. The prayer component is a time where group members will not just receive prayer, but also learn how to exercise Jesus' authority in their own lives and witness breakthrough in their circumstances.

This prayer time doubles as a ministry time, where believers are encouraged to flow in the gifts of the Holy Spirit. After the door is opened through worship, the atmosphere is typically charged with God's Presence. It is quite common for people to receive words of knowledge, words of wisdom, prophetic words, and for other manifestations of the Holy Spirit to take place in these times (see 1 Cor. 12). This is a safe environment for people to "practice" these gifts, take risks, etc. However, if there are individuals who demonstrate consistent disorder, are unceasingly distracting, have problems/issues that move beyond the scope of this particular curriculum (and appear to need specialized counseling), or have issues that veer more into the theological realm, it is best for you to refer these individuals to an appropriate leader in the church who can address these particular issues privately.

If you are such a leader, you can either point them to a different person, or you can encourage them to save their questions/comments and you will address them outside of the group context, as you do not want to distract from what God is doing in these vital moments together.

TRANSITION TIME

At this point, you will transition from prayer/ministry time to watching the *Supernatural Ways of Royalty* DVDs.

Group leaders/class teachers: It is recommended that you have the DVD in the player and are all ready to press "play" on the appropriate session.

VIDEO/TEACHING
(20–25 MINUTES)

During this time, group members will fill in the blanks in their participant workbooks. All of the information they need to complete this assignment will appear on screen during the session.

SCRIPTURE

We have selected a Scripture passage that accompanies the theme for the week. You or someone else can read this out loud.

SUMMARY

There is also short summary of the week's topic before the discussion questions. You can read this prior to the group meeting to provide you with a summary of that week's session.

DISCUSSION QUESTIONS
(20–30 MINUTES)

In the Leader's Guide there will be a number of questions to ask the group, most of which are in the workbook also. Some questions will be phrased so you can ask them directly, others may have instructions or suggestions for how you can guide the discussion. The sentences in bold are directions for you.

Some lessons will have more questions than others. Also, there might be some instances where you choose to cut out certain questions for the sake of time. This is entirely up to you, and in a circumstance where the Holy Spirit is moving and appears to be highlighting some questions more than others, flow in sync with the Holy Spirit. He will not steer you wrong!

Some of the questions will lead with a Scripture verse. To engage group members, you can ask for volunteers to read the Scripture verse(s). As you ask the question in the group setting, encourage more than one person to provide an answer. Usually, you will have some people who are way off in their responses, but you will also have those who provide *part* of the correct answer.

There is a very intentional flow in the order of questions. The questions will usually start out by addressing a problem, misconception, or false understanding, and are designed to take participants to a point of strategically addressing the problem, and then taking appropriate action.

The problem with many curriculum studies is in the question/answer section. Participants may feel like the conversation was lively, the dialogue insightful, and that the meeting was an overall success; but when all is said and done, the question, *"What do I do next?"* is not sufficiently answered.

This is why every discussion time will be followed with an activation segment.

ACTIVATION
(5–10 MINUTES)

- Each activation segment should be five to ten minutes at the *minimum*, as this is the place where believers begin putting action to what they just learned.

- The activation segment will be custom-tailored for the session covered.

- Even though every group member might not be able to participate in the activation exercise, it gives them a visual for what it looks like to demonstrate the concept that they just studied.

Goal

After the activation exercise, we have included a brief summary of the "Goal" from that unique session. This is what participants should walk away from each session knowing and applying.

Plans for the Next Week
(2 Minutes)

Remind group members about daily exercises in the workbook. Encourage everyone to participate fully in this journey in order to get the most out of it. The daily exercises should not take more than 15–20 minutes and they will make an ideal 40-day themed Bible study.

Be sure to let group members know if the meeting location will change or differ from week to week, or if there are any other relevant announcements to your group/class. Weekly e-mails, Facebook updates, and text messages are great tools to communicate with your group. If your church has a database tool that allows for communication between small group/class leaders and members, that is an effective avenue for interaction as well.

Close in Prayer

This is a good opportunity to ask for a volunteer to conclude the meeting with prayer.

THE IDENTITY OF ROYALTY

Prayer Focus: Ask the Lord to help every participant: 1) understand their identity as beloved, royal children of God, and 2) learn how to love others as they love themselves.

FELLOWSHIP, WELCOME, AND INTRODUCTIONS
(20-30 MINUTES—FOR THE FIRST MEETING)

Welcome everyone as they walk in. If it is a small group environment, as the host or leader, be intentional about connecting with each person as they come to the meeting space. If it is a church class environment, it is still recommended that the leader connects with each participant. However, there will be less pressure for the participants to feel connected immediately in a traditional class setting, versus a more intimate, small group environment.

In the small group, serve refreshments and facilitate fellowship between group members. In a class setting, talk with the attendees and ensure that they receive all of their necessary materials (the workbook and a copy of *Supernatural Ways of Royalty*).

Introduce yourself, and allow participants to briefly introduce themselves as well. This should work fine for both small group and class environments. In a small group, you can go around the room and have each person introduce him or herself, one at a time. In a classroom setting, establish some type of flow and then have each person give a quick introduction (name, interesting factoid, etc.).

Discuss the schedule for the meetings. Provide participants an overview of what the next eight weeks will look like. If you plan to do any type of social activity, you might want to advertise this at the start, noting that while the curriculum runs for eight weeks, there will be a ninth meeting dedicated to fellowship and some type of fun activity. However, you might come up with this idea later on in the actual study.

Distribute materials to each participant. Briefly orient the participants to the book and workbook, explaining the 15–20 minute time commitment for each day. Encourage each person to engage fully in this journey—they will get out of it only as much as they invest. The purpose for the daily reinforcement activities is *not* to add busywork to their lives. This is actually a way to cultivate a habit of Bible study and daily time pursuing God's Presence, starting with just 15–20 minutes. Morning, evening, afternoon—*when* does not matter. The key is making the decision to engage.

OPENING PRAYER

WORSHIP
(15 MINUTES—OPTIONAL FOR FIRST MEETING)

If a group chooses to do a worship segment, often they decide to begin on the second week. It usually takes an introductory meeting for everyone to become acquainted with one another and comfortable with their surroundings before they open up in worship.

On the other hand, if the group members are already comfortable with one another and they are ready to launch right into a time of worship, they should definitely go for it!

PRAYER/MINISTRY TIME
(5–15 MINUTES)

VIDEO/TEACHING
(20 MINUTES)

SCRIPTURE

There are three things that make the earth tremble—no, four it cannot endure: a slave who becomes a king, an overbearing fool who prospers, a bitter woman who finally gets a husband, a servant girl who supplants her mistress. (Proverbs 30:21–23 NLT)

Summary

In order to love others the way God calls us to, we need to love ourselves first. That's why Jesus tells us to "love others as we love ourselves." If we don't see ourselves the way the Lord sees us, we can't love anyone else; after all, First John 4:19 says "We love because He first loved us." Knowing the love of God for us as individuals is what transforms us and enables us to step out in love for others.

God's love for us isn't tied to our behavior or works. His love is who we are. But He uses His love to empower us so we can fulfill our destiny in Him. God wants us to come out of slavery and into freedom so we can lead others into the freedom He died for. Look at Moses, who lived among royalty with Pharaoh. God strategically gave Moses a royal identity so he would be able to free the Israelites from slavery in Egypt. Because Moses knew who he was—a royal son—he had the power it took to release God's people! Royalty had to be part of Moses' identity before he fulfilled his purpose because only people who are free can bring others out of slavery.

During these eight powerful sessions, Kris Vallotton will share the keys of knowing and stepping into your royal identity. Through biblical insights and personal examples from Kris' own life, you will be encouraged and empowered to live out your destiny as a beloved child. Take hold of how God designed you, step into the freedom of knowing you are loved and valued, and use your life to display the gift of Christ's love to those around you! It's what you were made for.

Discussion Questions
(25–30 Minutes)

1. God strategically placed Moses in the house of Pharaoh for a divine purpose. Why was it so important that Moses lived among royalty?

2. What does it mean to love others *as* we love ourselves?

3. What does it mean that we have a "scratch on our lens" when it comes to how we see ourselves?

4. How does knowing you are loved by God transform how you engage with the world around you?

5. Is it possible that God could be cultivating your identity before He releases you into your divine destiny? How are the two connected?

Have participants share personal stories (as they feel comfortable) of times in their lives when they struggled to believe they were loved by God. During these times:

6.   How was it difficult to love others?

7.   What did you do to hide or cover up who you were?

8.   How did God reveal His love and goodness?

ACTIVATION: TAKING HOLD OF YOUR IDENTITY

No matter where we are in life, it's never too late to renew our identity in the Lord. Jesus died so we would have access to God's love at all times.

Today, you are going to learn how to take hold of the identity for which God made you and how it correlates with the destiny He dreamt up for you at the beginning of time.

1.   Pray and ask the Holy Spirit to show you what your heart believes about your identity. Like Kris, do you see yourself as worthless? Or do you view yourself the way God sees you?

2.   Ask the Lord, *How do You see me?* Write down what you hear in a journal so you can come back to it.

3.   Commit to speaking this truth over yourself for the next eight weeks and believe in faith that God will cultivate the royal identity He's given you!

Ask if there are group members who would like to share what the Holy Spirit said to them about their identity. Have two to three people share.

The goal of this exercise is to recognize how God sees you—through the lens of His perfect Son, Jesus—and learn how to declare that truth over yourself. Faith comes by hearing, and only when we speak these truths out loud boldly will our hearts come to believe what God says.

PLANS FOR THE NEXT WEEK
(2 MINUTES)

Encourage everyone to commit to the activation exercise throughout the week.

CLOSE IN PRAYER

Video Listening Guide

A Prince or Pauper

1. Kris lost his dad at age <u>three</u> and didn't believe he was lovable because of the abuse he experienced with his stepfathers.

2. God encountered Kris in a dream reminding him of Proverbs 30, which says the earth cannot hold up under a <u>pauper</u> (slave) who becomes a <u>king</u>.

3. God renewed Kris' identity as a beloved child, inviting him to change from the inside out.

From the Throne Room to the Desert

4. Moses lived with <u>royalty</u> because he had to think like a powerful man who was free.

5. We must be <u>free</u> from slavery to <u>lead</u> others into freedom.

6. Jesus calls us to love others <u>as</u> we love ourselves. We can't love other people until we love <u>us</u>.

Relationships

7. Intimacy means "<u>into you I see</u>."

8. You'll never let anyone love you more than you love <u>yourself</u>.

9. When someone loves you more than you love you, you will eventually <u>sabotage</u> the relationship.

NOTES

THE CALL TO ROYALTY

Prayer Focus: Ask the Lord to help every participant: 1) understand their identity as forgiven, and 2) learn how to forgive others as they have been forgiven.

FELLOWSHIP AND WELCOME
(15–20 MINUTES)

Welcome everyone as they walk in. Be sure to identify any new members who were not at the previous session, have them introduce themselves so everyone is acquainted, and be sure that they receive the appropriate materials—workbook and book.

In the small group, **serve refreshments and facilitate fellowship** between group members. In a class setting, talk with the attendees—ask how their week has been and maintain a focus on what God *has done* and *is doing*.

Encourage everyone to gather in the meeting place. If it is a classroom setting, make an announcement that it is time to sit down and begin the session. If it is a small group, ensure everyone makes their way to the designated meeting space.

OPENING PRAYER

WORSHIP
(15 MINUTES)

When it comes to the worship element, it can be executed in both small group and church class settings. While a worship time is not mandatory, it is highly encouraged, as the fundamental goal of this curriculum is to foster each participant's increased understanding and outworking of the supernatural realm. This is where true, lasting transformation takes place. Worship is a wonderful way of opening each session and setting everyone's perspective on what the class is about—not accumulating more information, but pursuing the One who is at the center of it all.

PRAYER/MINISTRY TIME
(5–15 MINUTES)

VIDEO/TEACHING
(20 MINUTES)

SCRIPTURE

Then Peter came to Jesus and asked, "Lord, how many times shall I forgive my brother or sister who sins against me? Up to seven times?" Jesus answered, "I tell you, not seven times, but seventy-seven times (Matthew 18:21-22).

SUMMARY

God created each one of us for a powerful destiny. But living tied to the past keeps us from moving forward in what He made us for. How can we be released into the glory of our identity in Him? It all starts with forgiveness—forgiving ourselves and forgiving others.

In this session, Kris illustrates the power of our thoughts to either keep us chained to the past or move us forward into the future. Like Jacob in the book of Genesis, we have the opportunity to use our minds for slavery or freedom. While fixating on the pain of our past can hold us back from all God has for us, walking forward in forgiveness can free us and empower us. We are all manifestations of our imaginations, and living in forgiveness means we've responded to the vision God has given us instead of the ways others have wronged us.

But our ability to forgive isn't our own. We are only free to forgive ourselves and others because we have been forgiven by the King of Kings. He has washed us clean with His blood, equipping us to extend the same forgiveness to ourselves and those around us. In Him, we have power to forgive and live in the light of the destiny He designed for us.

DISCUSSION QUESTIONS
(25–30 MINUTES)

1. What is the difference between reacting to what we don't want to be and responding to the vision God gave us?

2. How does unforgiveness keep us tied to the past?

3. In Matthew 18, a king releases a man from his debts but puts him in jail when he does not forgive someone else. How does this story illustrate God's heart for forgiveness?

4. How are forgiveness and trust different? Does forgiving someone automatically mean we trust them?

5. What does Kris mean when he says "Forgiveness restores the standard"?

Have participants share personal stories (as they feel comfortable) about forgiveness.

6. Why is it so difficult to forgive someone who has wronged you?

7. Why is it hard to forgive ourselves?

8. How does forgiving ourselves and others equip us for our destiny in the Lord?

After people share their stories of promises fulfilled, transition immediately to the *Activation Exercise.* The goal of having people share testimonies of promises that have come to pass is to strengthen faith to engage the activation exercise.

ACTIVATION: FORGIVING YOURSELF FIRST

You are never too far gone. There's no sin too dark and no pit so deep that the love of God cannot reach you. Today, we are going to activate what we've learned and remind ourselves of the power of forgiveness in our lives, starting with ourselves.

1. Pray and ask the Holy Spirit to show you if there are parts of your past you don't feel forgiven for.

2. Examine your heart. Have you asked God to forgive you for these things? If not, take time to confess and repent before Him.

3. Take some time to journal. If you have already asked God for forgiveness, what is it about this sin that feels unforgivable to you?

4. Pray and ask the Lord to help you see yourself as a new creation, just as He does.

Ask if there are group members who would like to share what the Holy Spirit said to them about forgiveness. Have two to three people share.

The goal of this exercise is to examine your heart and discover how you've lived in unforgiveness toward yourself. When you operate in shame, you haven't stepped into the new identity Jesus purchased for you on the cross.

PLANS FOR THE NEXT WEEK
(2 MINUTES)

Encourage everyone to commit to the activation exercise throughout the week.

CLOSE IN PRAYER

Video Listening Guide

The Power of the Mind

1. What we <u>imagine</u> in our minds <u>manifests</u> in our lives.

2. We have been given a choice to <u>react to the past</u> or <u>respond to the vision of the future</u>. What will we choose?

3. Sometimes, <u>moving forward</u> into the future of our destiny <u>means forgiving</u> ourselves and others.

The Kingdom of God and Forgiveness

4. We are called to forgive <u>others</u> because we have first been forgiven by the King.

5. When Peter asks Jesus how many times he needs to forgive his neighbor, Jesus replies "<u>seventy times seven</u>."

6. The Lord can reach out and <u>forgive</u> us no matter how far we've gone.

The Meaning of Forgiveness

7. <u>Forgiving</u> and <u>trusting</u> are not the same thing.

8. When we truly forgive someone, we no longer have <u>permission</u> to hold their wrongs against them.

9. Before we can forgive <u>someone else</u>, we need to learn how to forgive <u>ourselves</u>.

NOTES

THE NAME OF ROYALTY

Prayer Focus: Ask the Lord to help every participant: 1) understand their identity as a new creation, and 2) live in light of how God sees them.

FELLOWSHIP AND WELCOME
(10–15 MINUTES)

Welcome everyone as they walk in. Be sure to identify any new members who were not at the previous session, and be sure that they receive the appropriate materials—workbook and book.

Encourage everyone to congregate in the meeting place. If it is a classroom setting, make an announcement that it is time to sit down and begin the session. If it is a small group, ensure everyone makes their way to the designated meeting space.

OPENING PRAYER

WORSHIP
(15 MINUTES)

PRAYER/MINISTRY TIME
(5–15 MINUTES)

Video/Teaching
(20 Minutes)

Scripture

Therefore, if anyone is in Christ, the new creation has come: The old has gone, the new is here! (2 Corinthians 5:17)

Summary

What's in a name? Names are more important than they might seem. When God invited Adam to name the animals, he was giving Adam the opportunity to co-create with Him, assigning both names and identities to His creatures. In the same way, we as children of God have the opportunity to co-create our reality. And believe it or not, it all starts with naming things.

The first step to taking on our royal identity starts inside of us. Many of us identify far too closely with lies about ourselves—for example, that we are sinners. Though we were once in sin, we are no longer identified by our wrongs. God not only forgave us our sins on the cross, He completely renewed our identity!

If we want to live powerfully in the royal identity God gave us, it is crucial that we ask God to renew our minds. Romans 12:2 tells us that all outer transformation starts with changing our thoughts. Once we grasp in our hearts and minds how God sees us—as new creations—we can step fully into the amazing destiny He has for us.

Discussion Questions
(25–30 Minutes)

1. How is it possible to live with names God did not give us?

2. How could calling ourselves "sinners saved by grace" be a lie?

3. How are we limited by the names we call ourselves?

4. What is the difference between conviction and condemnation?

5. What did John Maxwell mean when he said "You are not what you think you are or what others think you are, but you become what you think others think you are"?

6. What lies do you commonly believe about your identity?

7. What do you think God thinks of you?

8. How does adopting God's mindset about who you are change how you live?

ACTIVATION: WHAT DOES GOD THINK OF ME?

Stepping into our royal identity means taking hold of the name God calls us. Only when we come to believe His love for us will we live like the new creations He has made us to be!

If possible, have praise and worship music ready to go—either live or on some kind of audio system.

Encourage participants to pray and honestly list out the lies they have believed about their identity. Specifically, what names have they identified too closely with?

1. Now, take some time to journal and reflect on how those things affect your life.

2. Ask the Lord to give you a new name. How does He see you?

3. To activate your new identity in the Lord, write down what you heard (e.g. "You are _good enough_") and put it somewhere you can see it and declare it over yourself for the next week.

Critical It wasn't what was spoken its what wasn't spoken.

Ask if there are group members who would like to share what the Holy Spirit said to them about how God sees them. Have two to three people share.

The goal of this exercise is to transform how you live by renewing your mind about what God thinks about you. When we come into agreement with how God sees us, we will start to live like the royal children we are!

PLANS FOR THE NEXT WEEK
(2 MINUTES)

Encourage everyone to commit to the activation exercise throughout the week.

CLOSE IN PRAYER

Video Listening Guide

What's in a Name?

1. When Adam <u>named</u> the animals, he also <u>assigned them an identity</u>.

2. We have the same <u>power to co-create our reality</u> with God.

3. What we <u>call</u> ourselves and others affects how we <u>live</u>.

4. Many of us don't see ourselves how God sees us, as <u>new creations</u>.

A New Identity

5. God not only <u>forgave us</u> on the cross. He also <u>assigned us a new identity</u>.

6. We are no longer "sinners saved by grace." Instead, we are royal children of the King!

7. God does not see us in light of our sin, and neither should we.

Renewing the Mind

8. The most effective way to <u>change our lives</u> is to <u>change our minds</u> (see Rom. 12:2).

9. We are a human <u>being</u> before we are a human <u>doing</u>.

10. The new man not only has a <u>new name</u> but a completely <u>new nature</u>.

NOTES

TRAINING FOR ROYALTY

Prayer Focus: Ask the Lord to help every participant: 1) develop a culture that encourages a royal identity, 2) experience life-changing revelations and prophetic words about their calling.

FELLOWSHIP AND WELCOME
(10–15 MINUTES)

Welcome everyone as they walk in. Be sure to identify any new members who were not at the previous session, and be sure that they receive the appropriate materials—workbook and book.

Encourage everyone to congregate in the meeting place. If it is a classroom setting, make an announcement that it is time to sit down and begin the session. If it is a small group, ensure everyone makes their way to the designated meeting space.

OPENING PRAYER

WORSHIP
(15 MINUTES)

PRAYER/MINISTRY TIME
(5–15 MINUTES)

Video/Teaching
(20 Minutes)

Scripture

By this is love perfected with us, so that we may have confidence for the day of judgment, because as he is so also are we in this world (1 John 4:17 ESV).

Summary

When we develop a culture that brings out the greatness within us, we will start to live like the royal sons and daughters we are. Just like David's parents, we are called to promote a culture of raising others into royalty. Through prophetic words and revelations, we can gain insight on how God sees us and those around us!

One major key to setting up a culture of royalty is spending time in the Presence of Jesus. Spending time with Him is like looking into a mirror. When we behold Him, we become like Him. It's impossible to have a revelation about Jesus that doesn't radically change us from the inside out.

Though prophetic words are helpful tools in defining our destiny, to truly encourage us in living out our identity we need to create a prophetic culture. This means we not only hear what God has to say but obey it, and we allow Him to prune us into greater fruitfulness. Once we step into a place of obedience, we gain traction in our destiny, moving from slavery to friendship with God!

Discussion Questions
(25–30 Minutes)

1. What does it mean to develop a culture of royalty?

2. How did David and Bathsheba train Solomon in the ways of royalty?

3. How does being with Jesus change how we see ourselves?

4. What is the difference between prophetic ministry and prophetic culture?

5. How do we move from slavery into friendship with God?

6. How has spending time with the Lord affected your life in positive ways?

7. In what ways has obeying God impacted your life in Him?

8. What would happen if somebody saw greatness in me and began to call it out, to develop it in me?

ACTIVATION: THE 18-INCH JOURNEY

Sometimes, we know truths about our destiny in our hearts, but they haven't come into our minds. When dreams lie dormant in our hearts, chances are we won't act on them, which can keep us from the riches God has for us!

1. Pray and ask God to reveal to you treasures He's hidden in your heart. Are there dreams or ideas you haven't thought about acting on?

2. Now, take some time to journal about why you haven't lived out those dreams yet. Are you afraid? Do they seem too big?

3. Ask the Lord to speak into this vision. What promise does He want you to hold on to as you move forward?

Ask if there are group members who would like to share what the Holy Spirit said to them about awakening dreams. Have two to three people share.

The goal of this exercise is to move what's in our hearts into our heads so we can develop strategies and tools for living in our God-given destiny as we partner with Him.

PLANS FOR THE NEXT WEEK
(2 MINUTES)

Encourage everyone to commit to praying and reflecting on the activation exercise throughout the week.

CLOSE IN PRAYER

Video Listening Guide

Train Up a Child

1. David and Bathsheba <u>trained </u>Solomon in the ways of <u>royalty</u> from his birth.

2. The proverb "train up a child in the way he should go" refers to establishing a culture of <u>royalty and identity.</u>

3. Think of Proverbs as Solomon's homeschool textbook in the <u>ways of royalty</u>!

Jesus as a Mirror

4. When we spend time <u>with Jesus</u>, we will become <u>like Him</u>.

5. A new revelation <u>about Jesus</u> is a new revelation <u>about us</u>.

6. Looking at Jesus is like <u>looking into a mirror</u>.

Prophetic Ministry vs. Prophetic Culture

7. <u>Prophetic ministry</u> calls out our identity; <u>prophetic culture </u>develops it.

8. When Saul met the prophets, his entire <u>identity changed</u>.

9. Like Samuel's word to Saul, <u>prophetic words</u> call us into the people we are supposed to be.

NOTES

The Attributes of Royalty, Part 1

Prayer Focus: Ask the Lord to help every participant: 1) grasp the glory they were made for, and 2) move toward a new degree of glory in their lives.

FELLOWSHIP AND WELCOME
(10–15 Minutes)

Welcome everyone as they walk in. Be sure to identify any new members who were not at the previous session, and be sure that they receive the appropriate materials—workbook and book.

Encourage everyone to congregate in the meeting place. If it is a classroom setting, make an announcement that it is time to sit down and begin the session. If it is a small group, ensure everyone makes their way to the designated meeting space.

OPENING PRAYER

WORSHIP
(15 Minutes)

PRAYER/MINISTRY TIME
(5–15 MINUTES)

VIDEO/TEACHING
(20 MINUTES)

SCRIPTURE

I have given them the glory you gave me, so they may be one as we are one (John 17:22 NLT).

SUMMARY

To be made for royalty means to be made for glory. Before the beginning of time, God handcrafted you to be like Him, seated above all creation at His throne. We may suffer here on earth, but no suffering can be compared to the glory for which He is preparing us.

Though pursuing glory can sound self-focused, the truth is we are called into the glory of God. And because He gave us His glory when He gave us His Son, we are not at risk for "stealing" from Him. What's His has become ours! He delights in sharing His glory with us.

Another important aspect of sharing in God's glory is the role we play in renewing creation when we partner with God's destiny for us. Romans 8 tells us that all of creation longs to be renewed. When Adam sinned, all of creation fell under the curse. This means Jesus died to renew all of creation once again, and He chose to use us to make it happen. When we compromise and live outside of God's glory, we actually keep the world around us from being released from corruption. May each one of us find and run after the glory for which God made us, so all creation may rejoice!

DISCUSSION QUESTIONS
(25–30 MINUTES)

1. God longs to share His glory with us. Why are we so hesitant to pursue greatness?

2. How is our glory and the redemption of creation connected?

3. What does it mean to be "falsely humble"? Is hiding from our greatness the same as humility?

4. How does tying ourselves to a wrong identity affect everyone around us?

5. What does Kris mean when he says, "When a leader lacks confidence, the people lack commitment"?

6. Ask group members to share testimonies of a time you felt God's hand on your life in a certain area, but you were tempted to shrink back from it Share an example.

7. How did your living outside God's design for you affect you and those around you?

8. How did God awaken you to the glory you were made for?

ACTIVATION: MADE FOR GLORY

Living in light of God's glory means we come to terms with the greatness we were made for. This doesn't mean gloating in our own power, but partnering with God's power and using it to bring His Kingdom to earth!

1. Pray and ask God to reveal specific ways He has called you to be great. Parenting? Career? Friendship? A hobby or some other dream?

2. Now, brainstorm three practical ways you can use your glory in this area to show His glory to the world.

3. Ask the Lord to give you grace for this area of glory, and declare the truth about what He made you for throughout the week.

The goal of this exercise is to be empowered in the unique design the Lord has for our lives. When we walk with Him in His glory, we have all the tools we need to change the world!

PLANS FOR THE NEXT WEEK
(2 MINUTES)

Encourage everyone to commit to praying and reflecting on the activation exercise throughout the week.

CLOSE IN PRAYER

Video Listening Guide

Born for Glory

1. When we were young, we knew we were <u>born to be amazing</u>.

2. Culture <u>undermines</u> us; God wants to <u>unveil</u> us.

3. Our mistakes <u>don't keep us</u> from glory. Even when Peter denied Jesus, he became the rock on whom Jesus built His church.

Seated with Christ

4. God made us to be <u>seated with Christ</u> above all creation.

5. Jesus prayed in John 17 that we might <u>share in His glory</u>.

6. Living in God's glory is not stealing from Him; it's taking hold of <u>the inheritance</u> He died for.

Redeeming Creation

7. When we walk in glory, we play a part in <u>releasing creation</u> from corruption.

8. Adam's sin in Eden cursed <u>all creation</u>, and Jesus' death brought <u>full redemption</u>.

9. When we shrink back from glory, we <u>keep creation</u> from experiencing what it was made for.

NOTES

I exalt thee
citipointe worship
Higher wider deeper

The Attributes of Royalty, Part 2

Prayer Focus: Ask the Lord that every participant: 1) would learn the eternal value of honor, and 2) find practical ways to honor others in their lives.

Fellowship and Welcome
(10–15 Minutes)

Welcome everyone as they walk in. Be sure to identify any new members who were not at the previous session, and be sure that they receive the appropriate materials—workbook and book.

Encourage everyone to congregate in the meeting place. If it is a classroom setting, make an announcement that it is time to sit down and begin the session. If it is a small group, ensure everyone makes their way to the designated meeting space.

Opening Prayer

Worship
(15 Minutes)

Prayer/Ministry Time
(5–15 Minutes)

Video/Teaching
(20 Minutes)

Scripture

See, I will send the prophet Elijah to you before that great and dreadful day of the Lord comes. He will turn the hearts of the parents to their children, and the hearts of the children to their parents; or else I will come and strike the land with total destruction (Malachi 4:5-6).

Summary

Another core attribute of royalty is honor. While our culture tends to place an emphasis on youth, God's Word is full of reminders that He reveres those who have acquired His grace over time. That's why He says "gray hair is a crown of glory"!

When we reduce our sphere of influence to just one age or demographic, we miss out on the treasures others have gleaned in their lifetime. Accessing the grace, wisdom, and insight we need to move to the next level of glory may be as simple as an impartation from someone who has walked the path before us!

To live like the royal sons and daughters we are, we must incorporate honor into our lives. God designed His inheritance to be passed down from one generation to another. By unifying ourselves with other generations, we can paint a beautiful picture of His heart. So if you want to live in honor, first give honor!

Discussion Questions
(25–30 Minutes)

1. Can you think of any ways our culture emphasizes youth?

2. Why do you think God calls gray hair a crown of glory?

3. What's the difference between receiving grace through obedience/works vs. receiving it through impartation?

4.   Why could it be risky to limit revival to just one generation of people?

5.   What does it say about God that He values those who can no longer perform?

6.   Have you ever been tempted to reduce your sphere of influence to those nearest to your age?

7.   Have you noticed a difference in the grace you experience when you walk with a fuller view of honor?

8.   What does it mean to look to someone's spirit instead of their flesh? Do you have examples of both?

ACTIVATION: A CULTURE OF HONOR

If we want to receive grace to reach new heights of glory, we can start with looking to the generations around us—those who have already gone before us and acquired the wisdom and insight we don't yet have.

1.   Pray and ask God to reveal to you an area in which He wants to give you new grace.

2.   Now, journal and think of others around you who carry that same grace. *Lynn Potter*

3.   Go and connect with that person so you can glean the grace they've gathered through their lives.

Ask if there are group members who would like to share what the Holy Spirit said to them about honor. Have two to three people share.

The goal of this exercise is to grow in honor for those around us and be freshly equipped for the unique plans He has for our lives. There is grace for us to walk in!

PLANS FOR THE NEXT WEEK
(2 MINUTES)

Encourage everyone to commit to praying and reflecting on the activation exercise throughout the week.

CLOSE IN PRAYER

Video Listening Guide

Restoring Fathers and Sons

1. Elijah was called to <u>unite generations</u> by restoring <u>fathers to sons</u>.

2. Revival doesn't have a social class. God wants to pour out His Spirit <u>on all flesh</u>.

3. God hides the greatest treasures in the <u>twilight years</u> of people's lives.

Impartation and Reaping

4. If you live without honor, you relegate your life to <u>sowing and reaping</u>.

5. If you honor others, you can receive <u>impartations of grace</u>!

6. We can spend our lives toiling after something or <u>receive an impartation</u> through establishing a culture of honor.

Passing the Mantle

7. Elijah passed his <u>mantle of glory</u> to Elisha.

8. God reveres people who can no longer perform. It's these people who <u>impart grace</u> to others.

NOTES

Benjamin + John -
Matthew
Small group battle cry online
Joseph's podcast

Micah - School - Prayer for Lilly -

- Ariel -

(Nation)

Natalies

(Girl missing in Kgs mtn.)

Terry

Matt

The Authority of Royalty

Prayer Focus: Ask the Lord to help every participant: 1) celebrate their authority as co-heirs with Christ, and 2) live out the Great Commission by spreading His Kingdom to the nations.

FELLOWSHIP AND WELCOME
(10–15 MINUTES)

Welcome everyone as they walk in. Be sure to identify any new members who were not at the previous session, and be sure that they receive the appropriate materials—workbook and book.

Encourage everyone to congregate in the meeting place. If it is a classroom setting, make an announcement that it is time to sit down and begin the session. If it is a small group, ensure everyone makes their way to the designated meeting space.

OPENING PRAYER

PRAYER/MINISTRY TIME
(5–15 MINUTES)

VIDEO/TEACHING
(20 MINUTES)

SCRIPTURE

Then Jesus came to them and said, "All authority in heaven and on earth has been given to me. Therefore go and make disciples of all nations" (Matthew 28:18-19).

SUMMARY

When Jesus died, He stripped the enemy of his power and took the keys to hell. This is what it means that "all authority in heaven on and earth" has been given to Him. As His sons and daughters, we have inherited the same authority. Our primary task is to use His authority to bring Heaven to earth!

The Great Commission isn't just about getting people to Heaven. God certainly desires the salvation of His people, but He also wants to bring Heaven to earth. When we partner with Him in His authority, we can bring the powerful reality of Heaven into every aspect of the world around us.

Performing signs and wonders is one way to exercise our authority, but Jesus also asks us to be faithful and obedient in the small things. This is why Kris reminds us that "our seat of servanthood becomes our throne of glory." When we look for small, practical ways to show Jesus to others with our lives, He promotes us to a new degree of glory!

DISCUSSION QUESTIONS
(25–30 MINUTES)

1. What is the difference between the gospel of salvation and the gospel of the Kingdom?
   power and authority

2. How is our authority in Jesus linked with our role in the Great Commission? *- GO*

3. What does it mean to disciple the nations?

4. How can being faithful in the practical be a powerful way of bringing Heaven to earth?

5. After listening to this teaching, what misconceptions about the Great Commission may you have had?

6. How does understanding your authority affect your destiny in Him? What could it add to your life?

7. Have you experienced what Kris calls "being close to the palace"? How did it impact how you express the Kingdom to those around you?

ACTIVATION: THE GOSPEL OF SALVATION AND THE KINGDOM

God certainly desires that all His children join Him in Heaven. But another aspect of the gospel is bringing Heaven to earth. Partnered with Him, you can create a new reality around you!

1. Take some time before the Lord and pray about the authority you carry. What does the Lord want you to know?

2. Ask Him to reveal to you one way you can express the gospel of salvation to someone and one way you can bring the gospel of the Kingdom in that person's life.

3. Ask the Lord to give you practical ways to lead that person in a relationship with God and a new degree of freedom!

Ask if there are group members who would like to share what the Holy Spirit said to them about authority. Have two to three people share.

The goal of this exercise is to see the multifaceted nature of our role as co-heirs with Christ. When we partner with Him to bring salvation and freedom to the nations, His heart is revealed!

PLANS FOR THE NEXT WEEK
(2 MINUTES)

Encourage everyone to commit to praying and reflecting on the activation exercise throughout the week.

CLOSE IN PRAYER

WEEK 7

Video Listening Guide

Authority and the Great Commission

1. Jesus said "all authority on <u>Heaven</u> and <u>earth</u> has been given to me."

2. Because we are <u>co-heirs</u> with Christ, we have the same authority.

3. God wants us to bring <u>His Kingdom</u> to the world through the <u>Great Commission</u>.

Servanthood and Destiny

4. "Our seat of servanthood becomes <u>our throne</u> of destiny."

5. Faithfulness in the <u>small things</u> inspired the Queen of Sheba to promote her waiters.

6. In many ways, being <u>obedient</u> in the practical is as powerful as doing signs and wonders.

7. Doing <u>ordinary things</u> in a way no one ever has seen builds you the foundation to do <u>extraordinary things</u>.

NOTES

THE ASSIGNMENT OF ROYALTY: PRESERVING THE PLANET

Prayer Focus: Ask the Lord to help every participant: 1) see themselves as light in the world, and 2) bring that light into their neighborhoods, cities, and nations.

FELLOWSHIP AND WELCOME
(10–15 MINUTES)

Welcome everyone as they walk in. Be sure to identify any new members who were not at the previous session, and be sure that they receive the appropriate materials—workbook and book.

Encourage everyone to congregate in the meeting place. If it is a classroom setting, make an announcement that it is time to sit down and begin the session. If it is a small group, ensure everyone makes their way to the designated meeting space.

OPENING PRAYER

WORSHIP
(15 MINUTES)

PRAYER/MINISTRY TIME
(5–15 MINUTES)

VIDEO/TEACHING
(20 MINUTES)

SCRIPTURE

You are the light of the world. A town built on a hill cannot be hidden (Matthew 5:14).

SUMMARY

What does it mean to be the light of the world? In order for us to shine the light of Christ, we must leave the four walls of our church building and go into dark places. In Matthew 5, Jesus tells us that we are His light, to be shone in power around the world. When we adopt a "huddle mentality" and keep the light inside the church, however, the world misses out.

God intends to make all things new, and we are His partners in accomplishing this. But statistics show that cities with the most Christian churches actually have the most social problems. By partnering with God to bring the light of His Kingdom, we can set a new pattern. There is no end to the increase of His government and His peace!

DISCUSSION QUESTIONS
(25–30 MINUTES)

1. What does it mean to be the light of the world?

2. How is a basket over a lamp counterintuitive?

3. Why do you think cities with Christian churches are not yet experiencing the revival God has planned?

4. What does Kris mean when he says "we tend to see what we are prepared to see"? How can we change what we expect to see happen around us?

5. Has God ever convicted you of keeping His light to yourself or within your church?

6. How does understanding your role as light of the world affect how you engage with the world?

7. What are some practical ways you want to extend the reach of His light?

ACTIVATION: A CITY ON A HILL

God made us His light so He could put us on proud display! As royal sons and daughters of God, we are called and equipped to live boldly, shining for His Kingdom.

1. Break up into small groups of two to three and pray for each other's needs.

2. Ask each other for the areas that you are specifically wanting to grow in boldness in your city and community.

3. Follow the Holy Spirit's guidance in prayer, releasing strength over each other to persevere and endure.

4. Have each person share one practical way they can be that light to the people in their communities.

The goal of this exercise is to discover what it means to be the light of the world and define practical ways to live it out.

PLANS FOR THE NEXT WEEK
(2 MINUTES)

Let participants know that either this is the final week of the study or that you will be having some type of social activity on the following week—or at a specified future date.

CLOSE IN PRAYER

Pray that the group would truly be able to strengthen themselves in the Lord as they continue to daily walk out the tools that have been presented throughout the course.

Video Listening Guide

The Light of the World

1. In Matthew 5, Jesus calls us the <u>light of the world</u> and a city that cannot be hidden.

2. To live as light, we must go <u>beyond the four walls</u> of our church and move out into the world.

3. The <u>brighter</u> the light gets, the <u>better</u> the world gets until Jesus comes back!

Healthy and Whole Cities = Healthy and Whole World

4. The church was meant to bring <u>revival</u> to the world.

5. We are called to storm our communities with the <u>light and life</u> of Jesus in order to bring <u>revival</u>!

Getting People to Heaven and Heaven in People

6. Jesus talked more about getting Heaven <u>inside people</u> than getting people to Heaven.

NOTES

NOTES

NOTES

NOTES

NOTES

FREE E-BOOKS?
YES, PLEASE!

Get **FREE** and deeply-discounted **Christian books** for your **e-reader** delivered to your inbox **every week!**

IT'S SIMPLE!

VISIT lovetoreadclub.com

SUBSCRIBE by entering your email address

RECEIVE free and discounted e-book offers and inspiring articles delivered to your inbox every week!

Unsubscribe at any time.

SUBSCRIBE NOW!

LOVE TO READ CLUB

visit **LOVETOREADCLUB.COM** ▶